Colchester Castle

A history, description and guide

Colchester Borough Council
Published by the Recreation, Tourism and Arts Committee
Seventh Edition, 1989
ISBN 0 904394 04 2

The castle from the south-east

COVER: *The castle, from an oil painting by G. Miles, 1841*
TITLE PAGE: *Engraved lion by the entrance*

Contents

History	page 3
Description	page 13
Prisoners in the Castle	page 19
A Tour of the Castle	page 22

Key Dates in the Castle's History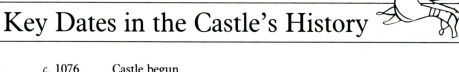

c. 1076	Castle begun.
1101	Granted to Eudes, steward of William I and II and Henry I.
1216	Besieged by King John.
1236	First mention of gaol; prisoners since before 1226.
1629	Alienated from the Crown.
1683	Sold to John Wheeley for demolition.
1746–67	Restored by Charles Gray.
1860	Museum opened.
1920	The castle acquired by town as a War Memorial.
1932–35	Castle court roofed.
1983	Conservation programme began.

If your time is limited, this may be read in conjunction with the tour on page 22.

THE HISTORY OF COLCHESTER CASTLE

The Building of the Castle

When the Normans first came to Colchester, they found a flourishing Anglo-Saxon town, surrounded by the still-standing Roman walls, which had been repaired by Edward the Elder (A.D. 917). At the time of Domesday Book (1086) there were 276 burgesses, and hence a conjectural population of some 2,000 people. Colchester was a valuable commercial centre and its position was one of strategic importance, having ready access to the south of East Anglia, and providing a good harbour, both for trading vessels and for warships, to protect the coastline and the Thames estuary. Thus, the town was an obvious site for a major fortress.

Within the walls various ruined Roman buildings must still have been visible, especially the great stone base (podium) of the Temple of Claudius (then perhaps known as King Coel's Palace), surrounded by the stone walls of its court, and offering, both by its position and the availability of its materials, a perfect defensive site. A ditch was dug around the outside, the earth being thrown over the crumbling Roman walls to form a mound topped by a wooden palisade, and within, the temple ruins were stripped to floor level and used as a base for the stone keep[1].

[1] See p. 13

The northern ramparts and ditch

Norman Knight

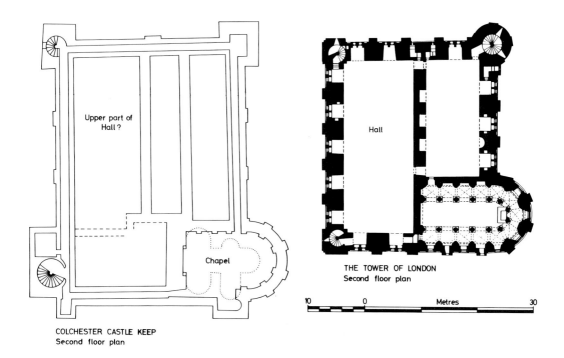

Comparative plans of Colchester Castle, and the White Tower, London

When this keep was only one storey high it was surrounded by battlements which can still be traced in the outer walls. Very soon, however, work was resumed and the building raised to a height of about 80 feet (25 m). The overall plan is so similar to that of the White Tower in London that it is likely that the architect to whom the latter is attributed, Gundulph, Bishop of Rochester, was responsible. Both designs probably owe something to Carolingian and Norman castles built elsewhere, and there is also a striking, but presumably coincidental, likeness to Seyhun in Syria, built by the Byzantines in the eighth century.

It is not known when building was commenced, but in the Borough Records there is a document referred to as the *Colchester Chronicle*. It dates from the fourteenth century but appears to have originated in St. John's Abbey a hundred years earlier. This states that the castle was begun in 1076. Recent criticism has suggested that there could be reasons for revising this date to 1074. It is known that Ralph of Norfolk planned a rising against William I in 1075, which was crushed, and this could provide a justification for either date. The castle is not mentioned in Domesday Book (1086) but this does not necessarily mean that it was not in existence.

It is also known that Cnut II, King of Denmark, contemplated an attack on England between 1080 and 1085, leading to William I implementing a 'scorched earth' policy along the east coast in 1085, an event which could be related to the construction of the battlements at first floor level as an emergency measure. Cnut, however, was murdered in 1086, after the great fleet, assembled for the invasion, had dispersed.

In 1101, however, Henry I granted the castle (*et turrim et castellum*, 'both keep and castle') to his steward Eudes. The King's steward (Dapifer) was a responsible officer, and Eudes had previously served both William I and William II in this capacity, receiving amongst other things the town of Colchester as a reward for his services. The grant, of which a copy survives in the Cartulary of St. John's Abbey, does not necessarily imply that building was completed, but it is a reasonable assumption.

In subsequent years the castle was steadily strengthened (a silver penny of Henry I was found in the northern ramparts) and though, with the consolidation of the kingdom of England, its military importance declined, the constable was frequently a person of distinction, as is indicated by the successive occupants of the office.

The Constables of Colchester Castle

The castle was throughout the Middle Ages a royal fortress, not a baronial residence, and hence was largely in the gift of the King. With it went the castle lands, and other major sources of revenue. The town of Colchester, given to Eudes and probably held before him by Waleran, 'an aggressive and unscrupulous Norman', and Walchelin, Bishop of Winchester, 'an extortionate underling', became the responsibility of the burgesses after 1189.

EUDES DE RIE, Eudo Dapifer (1101–20). Steward of the King. His family had been loyal supporters of Duke William; Eudes fought at the Conqueror's side at Hastings. He was tenant in chief of twenty-five Essex manors, and owned five houses, forty acres, and half the church of St. Peter in Colchester, where he seems to have been popular. He founded the Abbey of St. John, where he is buried, and granted the revenues of the castle chapel to the Abbey. He also founded the leper hospital of St. Mary Magdalen.

His only child, Margaret, married William de Mandeville, Constable of the Tower, who hoped to obtain the estates, but this would have made him too powerful, and Henry I probably appointed Eudes' sub-tenant HAMON DE ST. CLARE (by 1130). He may well have held the castle for King Stephen though it was bestowed by the Empress Maud on Aubrey de Vere when he could get possession of it, and perhaps also on Geoffrey de Mandeville, grandson of Eudes, who never apparently assumed his office.

HUBERT DE ST. CLARE (c. 1150) probably son of the above, was killed at Bridgnorth, 1155, while saving the life of Henry II. His daughter Maud (?) married William de Lanvalai I, Lord of the Manors of Stanway and Lexden.

From 1165 to 1190 the castle was probably in the sheriff's hands except for the period 1173–4 during the rebellion of the young King Henry II when Ralph Brito seems to have been constable.

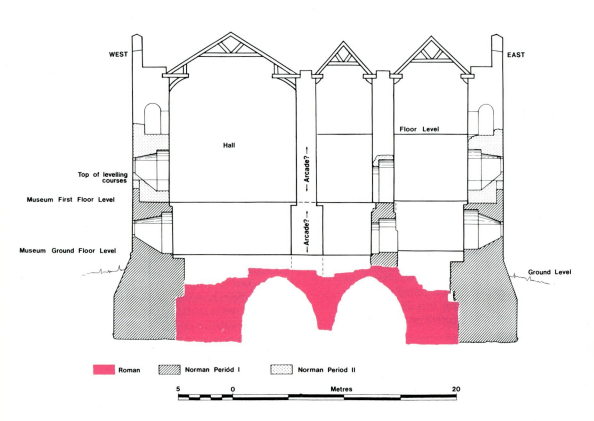

West–east section showing the castle surrounding the temple foundation

The castle was strengthened, garrisoned and victualled at this time but was not attacked.

JOHN FITZGODFREY held custody from 1191 to 1196 when he was succeeded by
WILLIAM DE LANVALAI II, who died in 1204. He was succeeded first by his widow Hawise and then by his son
WILLIAM DE LANVALAI III. The events of this period are of particular interest since William de Lanvalai was on the baronial side during the war with the King, though John had in fact stayed at the castle four times during his reign. Shortly after John's fifth visit in November 1214, the castle was entrusted to the Sheriff, Matthew Mantell, and John, suspecting his loyalty, sent Stephen Harengood, probably a Flemish mercenary, to take over the command, on 20 November 1214. He lost no time in placing the fortress in a state of defence. Eight ballistae (crossbows), two 24-inch and six 12-inch, were purchased, and trained engineers were sent from London in February 1215. The town was likewise fortified. Magna Charta was sealed in June, and Harengood subsequently had to return the castle to William de Lanvalai.

But the war was not at an end. King Philip of France sent a force to Suffolk in November 1215 to assist the barons, and some of them occupied Colchester castle. King John was besieging Rochester and it was not until 29 January 1216 that Savory de Meuléon 'the Bloody' began the siege of Colchester. He withdrew for a time when a baronial army threatened, but returned to the attack, and on 14 March the fiery King arrived in person. Within a month the French surrendered. A hundred and fifteen soldiers, including seventeen crossbowmen, marched away free, only to be arrested in London. Lanvalai was dispossessed, and Harengood restored. The French under Prince Louis again occupied the castle in 1217, but withdrew after the treaty of Lambeth (1217), and Henry III appointed
WILLIAM DE ST. MÈRE ÉGLISE, Bishop of London, followed by
EUSTACE DE FAUCONBERG (1223–27), also Bishop of London.
WILLIAM BLUND (1227–29),
RALPH BRITO (1229–30), and
JOHN DE BURGH (1230), who had married Hawys, daughter of William de Lanvalai III. She was buried in the chapter house of St. John's Abbey. He may never have had effective possession, and he and his father Hubert were ordered to deliver the castle to
STEPHEN OF SEAGRAVE in 1232.

During the ensuing years the appointments are frequent, some grantees apparently being intended to hold the castle in the King's name, and some being or becoming Sheriffs of Essex. The military significance of the castle was declining, and being replaced by its value as a prison and the status and revenue which its tenure conferred.

RALPH GERNON (1234–36),
HUBERT DE RUILLI (1236–   ),
RICHARD DE MONTFICHET (1242–46),
(?) RICHARD DE WHITSAND (–1251),
HENRY OF HAUGHTON (1251),
JOHN DE GREY (1251–55),
RALPH DE ARDERN (1255–56).

GUY DE ROCHFORD (1256–58), of Berden Hall was appointed by the King, but by the Provisions of Oxford the barons secured the appointment of
ROGER BIGOD (1258–62), Earl of Marshal of England and Earl of Norfolk. It then passed to the Sheriff and subsequently after the Battle of Evesham (1265) it was committed to
THOMAS DE CLARE (1266–68) and thence again to the Sheriff.

PRINCE EDWARD (1271) followed and his attorneys committed it to the Sheriff, and to
JOHN OF COKEFIELD in 1272.
JOHN DE BURGH (1273–74) was followed by two Sheriffs.
RICHARD DE HOLEBROOK (1276–c.1290) may have been followed by
ELEANOR OF PROVENCE (1290–91).

From 1297–1350 the Sheriffs were normally keepers, sometimes appointing a deputy. One of them William de Crepping, is recorded as having forcibly broken into a house at Fordham, robbed it and held the occupant to ransom.
ROBERT DE BENHALE (1350–c.1364), 'to be responsible for the prisoners' at a rent of £40.
LIONEL DE BRADENHAM followed until 1368.

In 1371 the last Sheriff withdrew and
GEORGE DE FELBRIDGE was appointed in 1376 at an annual rent of £10,
ROBERT DE VERE (1384–88),
SIR JOHN LITTLEBURY (1395),
ROBERT TEYE (1396).
HUMPHREY, DUKE OF GLOUCESTER (1404–47), was granted the castle by his father Henry IV while still a minor. His deputies included
  (i) William Dych who 'laid his hands illegally on Matilda Haras (of a wealthy local family) who was staying at the house of the aforesaid William, within the walls of Colchester, and without permission or warrant carried off the said Matilda to Colchester Castle and there cruelly imprisoned her, and placed thumbscrews on her hands till the blood oozed forth' (1406).
  (ii) William Bardolf, who in 1420 laid his hands on the Bailiffs and chief inhabitants of

Carvings in the east court, possibly made by French soldiers: fleur-de-lis, man with staff, and archer

the town while they were walking in all their finery one summer's evening on the Castle Hills, accompanied by their wives and daughters, and imprisoned them, presumably for ransom.

In 1447, Duke Humphrey died and the castle was first granted to
JOHN HAMPTON and two months later to Henry VI's queen
MARGARET OF ANJOU (1447–61), whose marriage to the King had been opposed by the Duke, but the custody of the castle continued under
JOHN HAMPTON until 1460. He was held responsible for escapes in 1455 and 1460. After the fall of the House of Lancaster, Edward IV appointed a Yorkist
SIR JOHN HOWARD (1461–85), created Duke of Norfolk 1483, who was killed at Bosworth Field.

THOMAS KENDALE (20 September 1485), a Lancastrian, received the castle and the Royal Demesnes 'for service as well within the realm as in foreign parts'. His deputy, William Derby, was pardoned for the escape of felons, 1487. He surrendered to
JOHN DE VERE, 13th Earl of Oxford (5 November 1496), of Hedingham Castle and constable of the Tower. He was confirmed in office by Henry VIII, 6 May 1509 in a document which brazenly claimed that the de Vere's title was hereditary and had been held since the appointment of Aubrey de Vere by the Empress Maud! His nephew
JOHN DE VERE (1513–26), a minor, was succeeded by his cousin,
JOHN DE VERE (1526–40), 15th Earl of Oxford. This individual 'commanded' Richard Antony, the elected Burgess for Colchester in the Parliament of 1529, to resign in favour of Richard Ryche, 'one of the Council of the said Earl'. The castle was later granted to his son-in-law,
SIR THOMAS D'ARCY (4 June 1541), who became Lord D'Arcy of Chiche (St. Osyth), replaced by Mary I with
ANTHONY KEMPE (1553), in whose time the Colchester Martyrs were confined and burned in

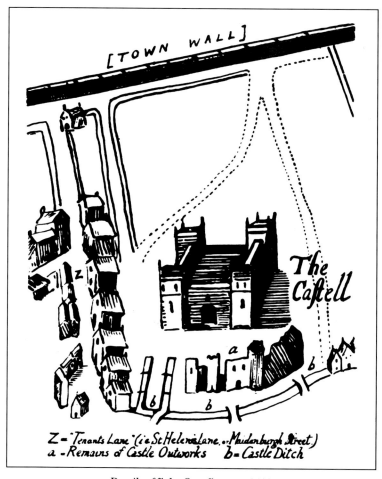

Details of John Speed's map, 1610

Prior's Prospect of Colchester, 1724

the castle. Elizabeth I replaced him with
HENRY MACWILLIAMS (14 December 1559), of Stambourne Hall, a Gentleman Pensioner of the Queen, succeeded by his son,
HENRY MACWILLIAMS (1586), killed in a duel on 8 June 1599. In his time the castle was visited by the topgrapher John Norden, who referred to it as being 'some tyme stronge and statelye, as the ruynes do showe'.

The custody for life of Henry's widow Mary Cheek was then granted to
JOHN LORD STANHOPE OF HARRINGTON (13 December 1599), M.P. for Northamptonshire and Treasurer of the Chamber, who had married the daughter of the elder MacWilliams; and thence to his son,
CHARLES STANHOPE (1603). The castle was alienated from the Crown in 1629 when Charles I granted the reversion of it to
JAMES HAY, EARL OF CARLISLE, whose extravagance led him to mortgage it.

After much litigation, the Stanhopes having lost everything in the Royalist cause, the castle was acquired by Sir John Lenthall (1649), and sold by him to Sir James Norfolk (1656), who had family connections in Colchester. He was forced to buy out Lord Stanhope's interest in 1662.

Charles Stanhope seems to have begun the demolition of the buildings in 1649 and this was continued by Sir James Norfolk.

He was succeeded in 1680 by his son, Robert, who built a row of houses over the ditch facing the High Street, which proved a ruinous investment. He therefore sold the keep, the only surviving building, to John Wheeley, a local ironmonger, in 1683 for demolition. The task proving too great, Wheeley eventually gave up and sold it in 1705 to Sir Isaac Rebow, a wealthy merchant and M.P. for Colchester 1692–1726. On his death in 1726 he devised it to his 'disobedient and undutiful' grandson, Charles Chamberlain Rebow, who quickly sold it to Mary, widow of John Webster and mother of Mrs. Sarah Creffeild, whose husband Ralph had bought the recently built 'Hollytrees' house.

Ralph was now dead, and in 1726 Sarah married Charles Gray, and Mary Webster gave the castle to her. Gray was a lawyer and later a trustee of the newly created British Museum.

The following year Mary Webster bought the castle bailey and some of the outer castle lands presumably also for the Grays, and when Sarah died in 1751 she gave the castle to Charles Gray.

In 1749–54 Charles Gray restored the south wing, using the services of a local architect, James Deane of Colchester. He created a library (the present lecture room) to house his own books, while he placed in the crypt the neglected library bequeathed to the town in 1630–31 by Archbishop Harsnett. Gray was one of the founders of the Castle Society, a group of gentlemen with antiquarian interests, and their library is still preserved in the Public Library.

On his death in 1782, the castle reverted to Mr. Round of Birch Hall, and remained in the possession of that family till, thanks to the generosity of Viscount Cowdray, it was purchased by the Borough in 1920.

During the Napoleonic Wars the crypt had been used as the armoury of the Colchester Volunteers (it still retains its steel-plated door). In 1855, Charles Gray Round made it available to the town as a home for the museum collection, which had been begun in 1846. This, combined with the collections of the Essex Archaeological Society, was eventually opened to the public on 27 September 1860. The record room was included in 1866 for the Borough muniments which remained there until 1985, when they were transferred to the Colchester branch of the Essex Record Office.

The museum grew steadily, but it remained in the crypt and library till in October 1931 the Roman vaults began to collapse through overstrain and exposure. They were reinforced by the then Office of Works, and the ruined building was subsequently roofed in, thus ensuring the protection of the vaults from the elements and extending the museum substantially.

During the 1939–45 war, the vaults were for a time used as an air-raid shelter, and a bomb fell, in 1943, in the bailey to the north, but did not explode.

Over the years, the steady deterioration of the outside walls has given cause for serious concern, and a thorough programme of conservation commissioned by the Borough was begun in 1983.

The castle in 1732, engraved by C. Vertue

The entrance doorway, early twelfth century

DESCRIPTION OF THE CASTLE

The original castle consisted of an upper and a lower bailey, each surrounded by a ditch and palisade. The palisade of the upper bailey was later replaced by a stone curtain wall and towers, with at least two gates, one to the south-west, and one to the west. The earthworks of the inner bailey still survive to the north, and the lower bailey ran northwards to the town wall. In John Speed's map of 1610 part of the wall and towers facing the High Street are shown as still standing.

The Castle Keep

Within the inner bailey was the **keep**, originally about 80 feet (25 m) high, the towers on the corners rising about another 10 to 15 feet (3·5 m). The towers project from the walls, which are also reinforced by flat buttresses, and on the south-east wall was a large apse, designed to accommodate the chapel. The dimensions are: north to south 151 feet (46·18 m), east to west 110 feet (33·5 m), and the thickness of the walls is 12 feet 6 inches (3·8 m) at the base. The foundations go down 12 feet (3·65 m) from the plinth and are 17 feet 6 inches (5·25 m) thick. The lower part was protected by a sloping apron, originally faced with ashlar (stone blocks), and the lower windows are all narrow slits opening into wide embrasures intended to admit light rather than to facilitate defence.

The **materials used** are bricks, septaria and dressed stones taken from the extensive Roman ruins available at the time of its construction. Septaria are clay nodules compacted by pressure in geological times, which occur in the exposure of the London Clays, especially on the coast near Harwich and Clacton, and were extensively quarried by the Romans. There is some Kentish ragstone and the dressed stones, mostly quarried in medieval times, came from Barnack in Northamptonshire and Quarr in the Isle of Wight, while fine white limestone from Caen in Normandy was imported for the reconstruction of the entrance in the twelfth century.

In the lower levels, while the materials were readily accessible, the masonry was laid in regular courses, bonded with Roman bricks, but above the first floor level the work deteriorates, perhaps because stones now had to be dug out of perished Roman buildings, and brick and ashlar are merely used for quoins (corner blocks).

It has recently been discovered that the courses of Roman bricks which are set vertically at around the first floor level contain units removed from

The battlements in the east wall, after K. C. Scarff

underfloor heating systems (hypocausts), which had been lifted intact, still retaining their Roman mortar.

Round the level of the first floor a series of **battlements** can still be traced (they are especially clear in the east wall and inside the garderobe [latrine] on the north-west stairs), and it would appear that when the building reached this height it was decided to put it into an immediate state of defence, but the work was shortly afterwards resumed, and the battlements incorporated. The design of the windows was also modified, but because of their greater distance from the ground they could safely be larger and so more useful. The corner turrets have a further set of battlements at a somewhat higher level, presumably in response to a second emergency.

In its original state the building comprised at least three storeys, of which only two now survive. The internal buttresses of the chapel were concealed by a tiled roof, added in the eighteenth century, and since this, on the parallel of the chapel in the White Tower can be assumed to have been about 30 feet (9·4 m) high, it has been conjectured that the third floor comprised the upper part of the Great Hall, with a pitched timber roof, protected by the outer walls to form a curtain. There is a passage in the thickness of the walls at this third level which extended all round the building.

The original **entrance** was from the platform which can still be seen under the bridge, reached from the ground by a timber stairway. From the platform the original doorway was possibly in the eastern wall of the projecting turret, necessitating a sharp turn to the right once inside the door. Since an armed man carried his shield on his left arm, this would expose him to attack should his presence be unwelcome. Alternatively, there may have been a smaller doorway in the south wall.

In the early twelfth century, however, this doorway proved inadequate, and a new and larger doorway partly made of Caen stone was cut into the south wall, while the side of the turret was refaced. The doorway led into a vestibule, with a seat for the guard. On the left a newel staircase, also reconstructed at this time, led to the upper floors. This, now called the **Great Stairs**, is exceptionally fine, with a diameter of 16 feet 4·8 m), the largest in Britain. The ashlar reconstruction was continued upwards until the stone was exhausted.

On the right was the **well-house**. The well is lined with septaria, which was originally faced with dressed stone. It is 5 feet (1·27 m) in diameter and over 40 feet (12 m) deep. The well shaft may possibly have been continued upwards to the first floor so that even if the doorway was forced the attackers could not readily molest the water supply.

Beyond on the left is an alcove, now called the 'Oven', probably intended as a guard chamber. Another arch led through a cross-wall into the central area, originally traversed by two parallel walls running north to south, one of which has now been destroyed and had its doorway at the extreme northern end. These walls divided the area into three long storerooms, and in the apse were two stone vaulted chambers, which were the prisons. The ground floor, of which a fragment has been preserved, was made of rectangular tiles. The floor above was of timber, for which the beam-slots can still be seen. The first floor had a similar plan, though possibly the western cross-wall was pierced at more frequent intervals. The room in the western section was probably the **Great Hall**. It has a set of three windows at the northern end. There are two large fireplaces and the hall would rise through the floor above, with a passage in the thickness of the wall at the upper level. The first floor would, therefore, afford accommodation for the garrison and maybe also the kitchen.

A Norman fireplace

The **fireplaces** are early examples of their kind, and discharge not through chimneys but through louvres about 18 feet (5·4 m) up in the thickness of the wall. The north-west turret, which is solid throughout the ground floor, was originally designed to accommodate two garderobes (latrines), one of which was subsequently blocked, and a newel staircase which led to the upper floors. At its foot there was a doorway in the north wall leading to a platform made by reducing the size of the turret at this point. It was probably intended to give access by a wooden staircase to the ground for which some blocked sockets are visible in the

The Great Stairs

outside wall. This would act as a postern in case of emergency. The apse at this level was occupied by the crypt or sub-chapel, which still survives retaining its massive barrel vaults.

Nothing is now known of the building above the second floor level save that the apse contained the chapel.

If, as discussed above (p. 14), the Great Hall extended through this level, the western cross-wall could have been pierced as an arcade leaving the easternmost section to be used for domestic rooms. The remains of one window are still visible at the northern end of the west wall and another in the north-west tower, showing that at this level the windows were larger than the slits below, since they could not readily be reached from the ground.

The lower part of the outer walls and buttresses of the **Chapel** survived the demolition. The massive buttresses suggest that it may have had two rows of columns with a passageway above, a design similar to that of St. John's Chapel in the White Tower. A small side chapel was constructed in the southern turret and this is also well preserved.

It would appear that the original floor was removed during Wheeley's demolition. A floor made of fragments of stone and brick was later laid, with two drainage channels leading to holes in the buttresses. The floor was clearly intended to protect the vault of the crypt below, and it was subsequently covered with three pitched roofs of peg-tiles.

When the conservation programme reached the south-east corner it was discovered that the roof timbers were seriously decayed, and their removal revealed the full size of the chapel. It was therefore decided that the roof should be reinstated in such a manner that this integral part of the castle could in future be seen by the public. A generous gift by Kent Blaxill and Company in commemoration of the 150th anniversary of the company, and a matching donation from the Association for Business Sponsorship of the Arts has made possible the present handsome structure, which it is hoped may later be linked into the east gallery by a new staircase. Meantime access is along the original passage constructed at this level in the thickness of the wall.

The Outer Works

(a) The Castle Ditch

The ditch has been shown by excavation to be over 70 feet (21 m) wide and over 16 feet (5 m) deep, the earth being used to form a rampart on the inside. It appears to have been constructed in two sections, the northern one enclosing the keep between its southern ends and then, not very long afterwards, an extension southwards to the High Street, which was curved inwards on its east side, for which the reason is not known.

The original approach from the High Street appears, from Speed's plan (1610), to have been through a barbican and gateway, whose lines are perhaps preserved in the S shape of Museum Street. Fragments of the walls have been located in the street and the site is marked by a plaque. The visitor then entered the bailey, and access to the keep was through a series of outer defences of which the foundations have been excavated.

(b) The Fore-buildings

The entrance to the keep was protected by a fore-building. In its earliest form this consisted of a massive wall enclosing the timber stairway to the entrance platform, with a doorway at the eastern end. In the later thirteenth century a larger building was constructed. It consisted of a gateway, flanked by two D-shaped towers, which led into a guardroom. The western wall contained a staircase leading to an upper level. A doorway to the east led to a passage which turned towards the keep and enclosed the earlier entrance. The series of narrow windows in the passage is puzzling, since they are so close to the ground as to constitute a danger to the defenders.

(c) The Bailey Chapel

The building, to the south of the keep, existed before the castle itself. It was originally built of timber with walls of wattle and daub, the inside being plastered and decorated with paintings. There is no evidence of date, but the mid or later tenth century is possible. Anglo-Saxon wall-painting is rare and it has been noted that the building is close to the site of the great Roman altar which stood outside the temple, raising intriguing possibilities as to the survival of some religious tradition. It has also been suggested that after the capture of Colchester from the pagan Danes by the Christian King, Edward the Elder, in A.D. 917 the temple court was used as some form of royal residence.

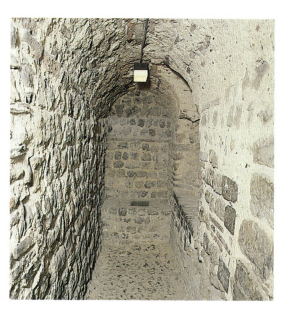

The latrine in the north-west tower

This timber building was later rebuilt in stone, and again rebuilt by the Normans. It had an apsidal (curved) eastern end, and when originally excavated there were holes in the walls, both inside and out, suggesting that they had been covered with marble cladding. In the early thirteenth century the north wall was rebuilt and a wall built across the apse, possibly indicating that the building was no longer used as a chapel.

Whatever the reasons, it is clear that this was a most sacred site, since the presence of a building so close to the keep would provide shelter for an enemy who had penetrated into the bailey.

(d) The Hall

A large hall, now beneath the rose beds, was built to the south-east, measuring 52 × 20 feet (15·85 × 6 m). It appears to have been begun at the same time as the castle, and fireplaces were added to it of the same construction as those on the first floor of the keep. At some time, probably in the thirteenth century, it was roofed with slates, an unusual material in this county. Its purpose is not known; perhaps it provided a residence for the constable.

A considerable number of skeletons were recovered during the excavations; in one grave outside the south-west corner of the chapel was one with another laid face downwards upon it. They date to the sixteenth or seventeenth century.

(e) Later Building

The only other structural alterations are the works carried out by Charles Gray in the eighteenth century; the well-house arcade and inner archway, perhaps with the entrance to the vaults and the ice-house therein (though the brickwork between the vaults seems to date from *c.*1710 and the ice-house could be *c.*1780), the doorway in the eastern wall, the cupola (1760), pantile roofs, the arcade on the first floor (1754–5), the windows in the south front and the study on the north-east tower (1746). He also built the temple-like wooden summer-house on the ramparts (1731) and the ruin, originally a rotunda, at the opposite end (1747). At some time in the eighteenth century or earlier, a house was built at the north end of the east court for the goaler. The present galleries were added in 1932–35.

The outer works after excavation, c. 1933

The gaol door, perhaps sixteenth or seventeenth century

Engraving of 1818 showing the former gaoler's house

Prisoners in the Castle

The earliest reference to a gaol in the castle is in 1236[1], but its use as a prison can be traced to c. 1226[2]. Two men charged with murder were released on bail in 1251 and references thereafter are frequent. Though most of its occupants were common felons, including pirates, some have been persons of distinction or historical significance, and there are records of various escapes.

An inscription by the entrance door commemorates Roger Chamberlayne, a former gaoler, and his wife Eleanor who succeeded him in 1360.

There is an account of a Trial by Battle in 1375 between John Huberd of Halstead and John Bokenham of Stansted. It was held in the bailey to the north. They fought in leather coats with staves piked with horn, and targets (shields), as was the custom. Bokenham was overcome and hanged.

In 1429 William Chivelyng, a tailor of Colchester, was convicted of heresy and burned before the castle, thus becoming the first of the Colchester Martyrs. A traitor who may have been one of the supporters of Jack Cade's rebellion was taken out of the gaol in 1450.

It is recorded that in 1454 a Sir Thomas Malory[3], was rescued from Colchester Castle by force. He was accused of various crimes of violence. The following year the roof of the gaol fell in, allowing the prisoners to escape.

[1] Close Rolls, 1234–37, 284.
[2] 5 Patent Rolls, 1225–32, 37.
[3] Modern criticism suggests that he was not to be identified with the contemporary poet and author of *le Mort d'Arthur*.

Scottish soldiers were imprisoned after the battle of Pinkie in 1547.

The persecution of Protestants did not really begin till 1555, though John Camper or one of his two companions had been executed in 1546. In 1555, John Lawrence and Nicholas Chamberlayne were burned and James Gore died in prison, doubtless in the castle, followed in 1556 by the burning of Christopher Lyster; John Mace, apothecary; John Spencer, weaver; Simon Joyne, sawyer; Richard Nichols, weaver; and John Hammond, tanner.

The next year, 1557, John Thurston of Much (Great) Bentley was arrested in March with his wife, and detained in the castle, along with John Johnstone of Thorpe, whose wife was dead but who was parted from his three young children. Thurston died a prisoner in the castle, but after several months' confinement his wife, Margaret; John Johnstone; William Bongeor, glazier; William Purcas; Thomas Benold, tallow chandler, Agnes Silverside, Helen Ewing, Elizabeth Foulkes, William Mount, Rose Allen, and Agnes Bongeor were burned, to be followed to the stake in 1558 by William Harris, Richard Day and Christiana George.

Under Elizabeth I, Catholics were likewise imprisoned, notably some of those who were concerned in the abortive rising of 1599.

Other Catholics were confined for seditous speeches in 1625. Protestant soldiers were confined after they destroyed the rails around the communion table (introduced under the High Church influence of Archbishop Laud) at Bocking Church in 1640.

Under the Long Parliament (1642) Alderman Benyon of London was confined at Colchester for voicing the disapproval of his colleagues in the City of London at Parliament's attitude to the King, where he was later joined by others of his opinion. Royalist prisoners followed after the taking of Croyland (Lincolnshire) by Cromwell (1643), and finally on 28 August 1648, Sir Charles Lucas, Sir George Lisle and Sir Bernard Gascoigne, the Royalist commanders who had held Colchester for twelve weeks against the Parliamentary forces under Sir Thomas Fairfax, were briefly confined, traditionally in the long vault to the east of the well-house. Gascoigne was reprieved, but Lucas and Lisle were shot in the castle bailey, where an oblisk now commemorates the event.

In 1653 three hundred prisoners were confined in the castle following the victorious war waged by the Commonwealth against the Dutch, and in 1665 no less than two thousand were brought to Colchester after the sea battle off Lowestoft, though presumably not all were confined here.

Intolerant of Catholics, the leaders of the Commonwealth were equally intolerant of their own extremists, and in 1656, James Parnell, then aged eighteen, after a scene in St. Nicholas' Church, was confined in the castle.

> 'where he was forced to lie down on the cold damp stones. Afterwards he was put into the hole in the wall . . . which was . . . about twelve feet high from the ground, and the ladder too short by six feet, he must climb up and down by a rope on a broken wall . . . for though his friends would have given him a cord and basket to draw up his victuals in, yet such was the nature of his keepers that they would not suffer it. Continuing in this moist hole, his limbs grew benumbed; and thus it once happened that as he was climbing up the ladder with his victuals in one hand . . . catching at the rope with the other, he missed the same and fell down upon the stones, whereby he was exceedingly wounded in his head, and his body so bruised that he was taken up for dead. Then they put him into a hole underneath the other . . . called the Oven . . . Here (the door being shut) was scarcely any air, there being no window or hole . . . and once, the door of the hole being open, and he coming forth, and walking in a narrow yard between two high walls, so incensed the goaler that he locked up the hole and shut him out in the yard all night, being the coldest time of the winter. This hard imprisonment did so weaken him, that after ten or eleven months he fell sick and died'.

A clearly biased coroner's jury agreed that he had committed suicide by refusing to take his food. (This account must refer to the present muniment room and the showcase in the entrance corridor below.)

For the rest, the castle continued as a gaol, incurring the strictures of John Howard, the great prison reformer, in 1780, by whom its revolting conditions were vividly recorded. Though defended by two local gentlemen in 1804, and partly reconstructed, its days were numbered, and the gaol was closed in 1835.

Archway on the first floor

A Tour of the Castle

If your time is limited, this account may be read in conjunction with the list of key dates. As a guide to the points of the compass, the present bookstall is in the south gallery.

You are now standing in the castle centre, which was originally divided by a cross-wall parallel to that surviving on the eastern side, making three parallel store chambers, lit only by the narrow windows, and hence very dark. You can see the slots for the roof beams below the gallery and in the east wall, where it changes from septaria (the local building stone) to a herring-bone pattern of Roman bricks. The castle owes its great size to the fact that it is built round the platform of the Roman Temple of Claudius, fully described in a separate book. The outer walls are some 12 feet 6 inches (3·8 m) thick. It is the largest Norman keep in England.

Under a sheet of glass to the north-east can be seen the only surviving portion of the original floor made of coarse tiles. Traces of the second cross-wall can be seen in the northern wall, which was pierced by a doorway at its point of junction.

The vault which now houses the display relating to the siege is original and near its entrance the remains of the second north–south wall may be seen. Within, in the right hand (north-west) corner is a cross carved on one of the stones. This vault is by tradition the place in which the Royalist commanders during the Siege of Colchester were briefly confined before their execution in the outer bailey on 28 August 1648.

Ascend the stairs to the first floor. In the alcove to the right was formerly a doorway leading to a platform from which a wooden stairway led to the ground. In the turret a staircase rises from this level to the upper floors. Walk down the gallery on the western side, passing two of the great fireplaces, and look back from the southern end. You are now on the original first floor level, where the windows are more frequent, though there was again a cross-wall on the same line as the one below, though this was perhaps pierced with arches. This was probably the Great Hall, extending upwards through another storey, where there was a passage in the thickness of the outer wall. It would have had an open timber roof.

Remains of the floor in the court

The court to the north before 1932 showing herring-bone masonry
The court to the south before 1932 showing Gray's arcade

Behind you is the arcade constructed in the eighteenth century by Charles Gray, to give access to the crypt and his library when the rest of the castle was a ruin. A passage leads to the Great Stairs and the alcove at the end was intended for the portcullis winch.

Walk through the arcade to the crypt (more correctly, the sub-chapel), which retains its original vaults, some of the oldest in the country. When it was built it was only lit by slit windows, of which two survive; the remainder were enlarged by Gray in the eighteenth century. The plaster was possibly decorated with wall paintings.

The showcase in the northern bay is constructed in an original opening, later partly blocked. Its function is not known.

Above the crypt is the chapel (see p. 16) which may be visited on guided tours.

Turn into the east gallery, whence a staircase leads down to the cells*. The present prison doorway may well be as old as the sixteenth century, or even older, and again the original narrow windows have been replaced. There is a small lobby and fireplace for the gaoler, and the two vaulted cells are original with wooden partitions, built in the early eighteenth century. There were formerly three other cells in the main section.

Returning to the gallery, there are two further fireplaces and a latrine in the thickness of the wall. There may have been private apartments here with those of the constable on the floor above, adjacent to the chapel. Turn left through the archway, down the stairs and go out to the main entrance. On the left is the entrance to the vaults* and the arcade built by Charles Gray for the well-house. The well is over 40 feet (12 m) deep. On the right is the so-called 'Oven', the prison of James Parnell, the first Quaker martyr, and the entrance to the Great Stairs*. There are two interesting scratched drawings of a Norman soldier and a horseman on the northern wall of the access passage.

*Admission by appointment or in guided tours.

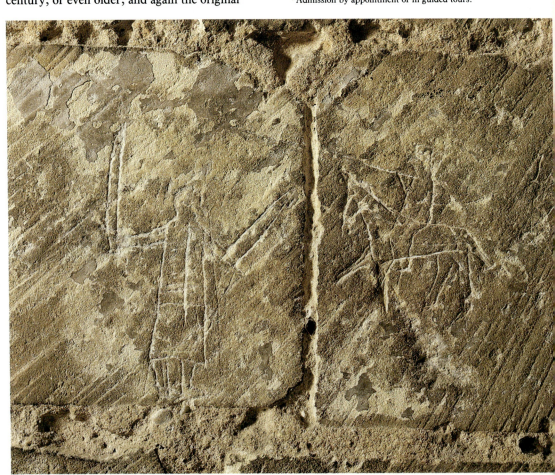

Norman soldier and knight on the Great Stairs

Carving of St. Christopher by the entrance door

Drawing by John Constable, c. 1813

Behind the entrance doors are the slot for the door-bar and a number of carvings in the niche probably done by guards to pass away the time. St. Christopher carrying the infant Jesus, and two other figures, one a bishop, can be made out, and to the left is an inscription referring to Roger Chamberlayne and his wife[1]. He has been identified with a burgess admitted in 1347–48 who may have been gaoler in the castle, being succeeded by his wife Eleanor in 1360. Both were fined by the Borough for offences connected with the sale of beer.

Outside, the bridge crosses over the foundations of the thirteenth-century outer works for the defence of the gate, which have been excavated to the original level. The particularly complex entrance ensured that any attacker would have to pass round three right-angles before approaching the entrance doors. The main archway is of the early twelfth century and replaces an earlier and smaller one; the groove for the portcullis can also be seen.

To the left can be seen the foundations of the bailey chapel with an apsidal (curved) end, subsequently walled off, and of very early date (see p. 16).

The exterior of the castle is particularly fine, and it should be remembered that the original building was almost half as high again as it now is. The great windows in the south front and the apse were added in the eighteenth century along with the cupola over the Great Stairs. On the top of the small and solid tower which protects the entrance is a sycamore tree, traditionally planted by the daughter of the then Mayor of Colchester to commemorate the battle of Waterloo (1815).

[1] The inscription reads: Al yat [pray] for Roger/Chambyrleyn/& for hys wyf God/[g]ef hem a gode/lyf.

Constable sketched the castle from exactly this position

The keep was originally surrounded by a wall and ditch now covered by the buildings to the south. The original gateway was probably in Museum Street and there was another gate on the north-western side of the bailey.

Walking round the building, the battlements of the castle's first period can still be made out, especially on the east side, at first floor level, also the latrine shoots. The slit windows are almost all original and the two types, larger and smaller, can be clearly distinguished.

At the rear (north) is the great rampart of the inner bailey, built over the Roman buildings of the court of the Temple of Claudius. It now bears a summer-house and the ruins of a rotunda built in the eighteenth century by Charles Gray.

The Lucas Vault